MICHELANGELO

SCULPTOR AND PAINTER

SPECIAL LIVES IN HISTORY THAT BECOME

Signature LIVES

MICHELANGELO

SCULPTOR AND PAINTER

by Barbara A. Somervill

Content Adviser: Paul Barolsky, Ph.D.,
Commonwealth Professor of Art History,
University of Virginia

Reading Adviser: Rosemary G. Palmer, Ph.D.,
Department of Literacy, College of Education,
Boise State University

COMPASS POINT BOOKS  MINNEAPOLIS, MINNESOTA

Compass Point Books
3109 West 50th Street, #115
Minneapolis, MN 55410

Visit Compass Point Books on the Internet at *www.compasspointbooks.com*
or e-mail your request to *custserv@compasspointbooks.com*

Editor: Jennifer VanVoorst
Lead Designer/Page Production: Jaime Martens
Photo Researcher: Svetlana Zhurkina
Cartographer: XNR Productions, Inc.
Educational Consultant: Diane Smolinski

Managing Editor: Catherine Neitge
Art Director: Keith Griffin
Production Director: Keith McCormick
Creative Director: Terri Foley

Library of Congress Cataloging-in-Publication Data
Somervill, Barbara A.
  Michelangelo: sculptor and painter / by Barbara A. Somervill.
     p. cm. — (Signature lives)
  Includes bibliographical references and index.
  ISBN 0-7565-0814-2 (hardcover)
  1. Michelangelo Buonarroti, 1475–1564—Juvenile literature.
  2. Artists—Italy—Biography—Juvenile literature. I. Title. II. Series.
  N6923.B9S5 2005
  709'.2—dc22   2004017116

Signature Lives

RENAISSANCE ERA

The Renaissance was a cultural movement that started in Italy in the early 1300s. The word *renaissance* comes from a Latin word meaning "rebirth," and during this time, Europe experienced a rebirth of interest and achievement in the arts, science, and global exploration. People reacted against the religion-centered culture of the Middle Ages to find greater value in the human world. By the time the Renaissance came to a close, around 1600, people had come to look at their world in a brand new way.

Table of Contents

1 THE SCULPTOR PAINTS

⌒⊷⊶⌒

Michelangelo perched on a scaffold 60 feet (18 meters) above the floor of the Vatican's Sistine Chapel. He mixed the thin plaster coat that would be the base for the next section of his ceiling fresco. Gently, he smoothed the plaster over the rough ceiling surface. He traced his original drawing onto the plaster. He began painting the hand of God.

Down below, Pope Julius II paced the chapel floor. He was anxious for Michelangelo to finish. Michelangelo had started the project four years before, in 1508. Then, Michelangelo had been 33 years old and strong from years of carving stone. Yet, throughout the years of painting, he complained of aches, discomfort, tired bones, and feeling old. Perhaps he complained so much because he hated

Although Michelangelo didn't think of himself as a painter, he is most often remembered for painting the ceiling frescoes of the Vatican's Sistine Chapel.

painting. He was a sculptor; he worked in stone. Painting was simply not what Michelangelo wanted to do.

Now, it was the fall of 1512. Pope Julius wanted the work done. The pope was dying, and the ceiling fresco was a dream he wanted fulfilled before he died. Every day the pope shouted up to Michelangelo, asking when he would be finished. Michelangelo didn't have an answer.

Up on the scaffold, Michelangelo added minerals to his mortar and ground the pigments for his paint. Cinnabar made a rich, deep red. Azurite or lapis lazuli gave sky blues. Yellow and red ochre were Italy's natural earthtones. Green from copper, black from burnt almond stones, purples from plum juice—Michelangelo mixed the colors of life from these basic pigments. Slowly, he painted God's hand and poured life into Adam. He twisted a serpent around a tree, tempting Adam and Eve. He added rosy cheeks to the faces of sibyls and grizzled beards to ancient prophets.

But painting the Sistine Chapel's ceiling was not quick or easy. And Michelangelo had his own speed of working. After all, he was a sculptor, not a painter. He had grumbled when the pope had assigned him the job. He grumbled daily as he climbed the scaffold to work.

Unlike many fresco artists, Michelangelo did all his own painting. Possibly, he thought no other artist could paint like him. More likely, he was unsure of his skills. He didn't want to embarrass himself by making mistakes in front of other artists.

Although he had been an apprentice to a fresco painter, he had paid little attention to his studies. For the chapel ceiling, he learned by trial and error how to mix the thin plaster base. He spent long hours grinding pigments and trying out colors.

This portrait of Michelangelo was painted by his contemporary, Jacopino del Conte.

Although Michelangelo complained that he would have liked to work further on the ceiling, the scaffolding finally came down. The pope had his ceiling. For nearly 500 years, people have stood in the chapel and gazed in awe at Michelangelo's artistry.

Michelangelo was a true Renaissance man. He carved statues so beautiful that the stone seemed alive. He designed buildings and public squares. He built walls to protect the city of Florence from attack. He wrote poetry. Despite these many gifts, people most often remember Michelangelo for the project he hated the most—the Sistine Chapel ceiling fresco. ❧

2 CHAPTER

AN ARTIST BORN

⊱⊰

Michelangelo's Italy was not the same Italy found on today's globe. In the 15th and 16th centuries, Italy was a collection of small republics, states governed by the pope, and city-states. Republics covered central cities and the surrounding countryside. Such republics included Florence, Genoa, and Venice. Each had its own governors, nobles, peasants, merchants, priests, and government officials.

One such official was Lodovico di Lionardi Buonarroti Simoni. His family had a good, noble name but no money to back it up. So, Lodovico had to work for a living. He served as an official with the duty to convict and sentence criminals. One assignment took Lodovico, his very pregnant wife, and 2-year-old son to Caprese and Chiusi for a six-month stay.

Although he soon moved to the city of Florence, Michelangelo spent his early years in the Italian countryside.

Holy Roman Empire
Map shows boundaries of 1500.

SWISS CONFEDERATION
TYROL
CARNIOLA
Duchy of Savoy
Duchy of Milan
KINGDOM OF FRANCE
KINGDOM OF HUNGARY
REPUBLIC OF VENICE
Adriatic Sea
Settignano
Florence
Florence • Caprese
REPUBLIC OF GENOA
Rep. of Siena
PAPAL STATES
OTTOMAN EMPIRE
Corsica
KINGDOM OF NAPLES
N W E S
Sardinia
Tyrrhenian Sea
Ionian Sea
ASIA
EUROPE
KINGDOM OF ARAGON
Mediterranean Sea
Sicily
AFRICA
0   100 miles
0   100 kilometers

In Michelangelo's time Italy was made up of a number of republics, city-states, and papal states.

Caprese was a remote region in the Apennine Mountains in central Italy. Small villages were nestled deep in the fertile valleys, and farms dotted the rugged, stony hillsides. Rows of neatly tended grapes filled small vineyards. Sheep grazed on the open hillsides. The Arno River wound its lazy way through Caprese toward the Mediterranean Sea.

It was in Caprese that Francesca di Neri Buonarroti gave birth to her second son, Michelangelo di Lodovico di Lionardo Buonarroti Simoni, on March 6, 1475. Michelangelo would be the second of five sons. Lionardo was the eldest, followed by Michelangelo, Buonarroto, Giovansimone, and Gismondo.

After six months in Caprese, Lodovico and his family returned to Florence. He bought a small farm near the village of Settignano. As an infant, Michelangelo lived with a wet nurse in the village. It was a common practice in Florence at that time to place a child with a nurse for his or her first few years. Michelangelo's wet nurse was the wife and daughter of stonecutters. He once said, "From my nurse I got the chisel and hammer with which I make my figures."

At about 3 years old, Michelangelo returned to live with his family. By that time, his brother Buonarroto was an infant, and Giovansimone was on the way. The household was crowded and poor. Lodovico earned little as a government employee, and his farm was not overly productive. Farming was hard work, and Lodovico believed such effort to be beneath him.

The city of Florence is named after a Latin word that means "blossoming." It was here that the Renaissance movement blossomed, and the city was home to many important figures of this time. Among them were the painters Leonardo da Vinci and Giovanni Bellini, the writers Dante Alighieri and Giovanni Boccaccio, and the astronomer Galileo.

At the age of 6, Michelangelo lost his mother. Francesca died in 1481, leaving behind five young sons, including a newborn, for Lodovico to raise.

In 1485, Lodovico sent 10-year-old Michelangelo to Latin school to learn reading, writing, and mathematics. It is easy to imagine Michelangelo bored with Latin verbs and doodling pictures on his papers. Artistic talent drove Michelangelo from an early age, much to his father's dismay. Lodovico considered art a form of manual labor, like plumbing, farming, or carpentry. He had hoped his sons would pursue professions that didn't require getting one's hands dirty. However, there was no arguing with talent. Michelangelo's desire to draw controlled his future. Art was his destiny.

Finally, Lodovico gave in. He signed a contract to make Michelangelo an apprentice in the Currado family. The contract read:

> *I record this first of April [1488] how I, Lodovico di Lionardo di Buonarrota, bind my son Michelangelo to Domenico and Davit de Tommaso di Currado for the next three ensuing years, under these conditions and contracts: to wit, that the said Michelangelo shall stay with the above-named masters during this time, to learn the art of painting and to practice the same, and to be at the orders of the above-named...*

And so Michelangelo embarked on a career as a painter's apprentice. Domenico di Currado was better known by the name Ghirlandaio. He earned this name because he crafted the gold and silver garlands that were often worn by Florentine noblewomen for special events. He also painted garlands on the hair of his female subjects.

Ghirlandaio and his brothers had a thriving family business. The three brothers—Domenico, Davit, and Benedetto—painted frescoes. They received many of their projects from the Roman Catholic

This painting, The Marriage of Mary, was painted by Domenico Ghirlandaio.

Church, while others were painted in government buildings or for wealthy patrons.

As an apprentice, Michelangelo was supposed to learn the various techniques of fresco painting. To begin, he was given a sketchbook and told to copy work previously drawn by Ghirlandaio. Young Michelangelo had an abundance of talent, but he was also stubborn and quite full of himself. He believed his drawings were better than his master's and said so. Domenico Ghirlandaio admitted that Michelangelo had an excellent memory for detail and a sharp eye for drawing. However, the apprentice irritated the master with his attitude.

Michelangelo lacked the patience to learn the craft of painting frescoes. He showed little interest in grinding or mixing colors. He didn't want to mix the various ingredients needed for the smooth plaster needed for fresco painting.

At 14, Michelangelo copied several of Ghirlandaio's drawings of women. He dared to "correct" Ghirlandaio's own drawings by going over them with a broad-nibbed pen. Michelangelo showed the women as they should have been drawn. Clearly, Michelangelo's artistry was the greater, but he lacked tact. The pupil shamed his master, and the master had had enough. Michelangelo needed to find a new patron. Ghirlandaio claimed there was no teaching the know-it-all Michelangelo.

This illustration from the 16th century shows a painter's apprentice grinding pigments.

It was about this time that Michelangelo realized that paint and plaster were not for him. He believed painting was a lesser form of art, relying as it did on color rather than form. He wanted to work in stone, study the human figure, and produce fine sculptures. Michelangelo's next step took him into the world of true Florentine nobility—the palace of the Medici. ℘

VIRTVTV
OMNIV
VAS

VITI
VTI
C

3 THE GARDEN OF THE MEDICI

❧∾⌘∾☙

During the Renaissance, Florence thrived under the gentle rule of the Medici family. The Medici were bankers and merchants at the highest level. They built hospitals, libraries, and museums for Florence. They supported artists, poets, philosophers, and scientists. They considered themselves "friends to the people," a title that rankled the hearts of their enemies.

In the early 1400s, Cosimo de Medici solidified the family's power in Florence and the surrounding region. There, he built a palace for his family where royalty and artists alike were invited to dine. The palace, with its open courtyard, sweeping marble staircases, and soaring columns became a seat of learning.

In 1490, Lorenzo de Medici was the head of the family. The Medici had become the wealthiest family

Lorenzo de Medici, head of Florence's powerful Medici family, was one of Michelangelo's early patrons.

The city of Florence was filled with beautiful waterways, churches, and homes.

in Italy. At the Medici palace lived family, distant relatives, servants, artists, and many of the greatest minds of Italy.

Lorenzo de Medici was called "the Magnificent." He met the obligations of one with great wealth, supporting many relatives, providing dowries to marry off poor female relations, and setting up young men in business. He exerted influence in all aspects of Florentine society, culture, and politics.

Michelangelo and Lorenzo de Medici were distantly related through Michelangelo's grandmother.

So, Michelangelo's father appealed to Lorenzo to take his son as an apprentice artist. Lorenzo, used to pleas from poor relatives, listened to Lodovico. He asked the father what he wanted for himself, but Lodovico wanted only a small job to help the family finances. Lorenzo expected a larger, bolder request.

And so, at the age of 15, Michelangelo entered the world of the Medici. He lived at the palace, most likely in a small servant's room. Along with hundreds of others, he ate at the Medici table. And in the Medici garden of Piazza San Marco, he practiced sculpting—a difficult and demanding art. Sculpting requires striking hammer against chisel in exactly the right place—and doing it several thousand times. The well-directed chisel chips away a sliver, a flake, or a speck of stone at a time. Too much chipped away in one place or another destroys the shape of the sculpture. One serious missed hit and the stone is worthless. Another badly placed blow might reveal faults, veins, or

The great artist and scientist Leonardo da Vinci once described the life of a sculptor: "The sculptor in creating his work does so by the strength of his arm by which he consumes the marble…and this is done by most mechanical exercise, often accompanied by great sweat which mixes with the marble dust and forms a kind of mud daubed all over his face. The marble dust flours him all over so that he looks like a baker; his back is covered with a snowstorm of chips, and his house is made filthy by the flakes and dust of stone."

Michelangelo practiced sculpting in the beautiful Medici gardens.

cracks within the marble. All in all, sculpting is a very difficult business.

His new life as a sculptor in the Medici garden truly inspired Michelangelo. He became friends with

Lorenzo the Magnificent's children, nephews, and nieces. Lorenzo's son Giovanni and his nephew Giulio would eventually become two of Michelangelo's most valued patrons. Giovanni later became Pope Leo X in 1513, and Giulio was elected Pope Clement VII in 1523. As young men, however, they enjoyed the atmosphere of the Medici palace and the friendships of writers, artists, and scientists.

Michelangelo studied classic Greek and Roman sculptures in the Medici garden. The garden was an artist's dream. Surrounded by high walls, it was protected from nosy onlookers and city noise. Several work areas, called loggias, provided places for up-and-coming sculptors to practice. Michelangelo learned to use the hammer and chisel. He was more successful than most beginning sculptors, and this success made others jealous. Pietro Torrigiano, another budding sculptor, envied Michelangelo's talent. In a fit of jealousy, he struck Michelangelo and broke his nose.

In 1491, everything in Michelangelo's life seemed perfect. He enjoyed the patronage of the most powerful and wealthiest man in Florence. He lived in

> *The Medici family held great power in Florence, and their influence eventually spread throughout Italy and the rest of Europe. Three members of the Medici family were elected pope, and two women became queens of France, where they adopted the French spelling of their name, de Medicis.*

comfort and dined among the greatest minds of his time. At work, he could study some of the finest sculpture available at the Medici Garden. His hammers, chisels, and stone were supplied for him. Plus, he received a salary of five ducats a week—a fortune for someone who grew up in his father's meager household.

During the time he lived at the Medici residence, Michelangelo produced two sculptures: *Madonna of the Stairs* and *Battle of the Centaurs*. The *Madonna* is probably Michelangelo's earliest work still in existence. The piece measures 1.3 feet (40 centimeters) by 1.8 feet (55 cm) and is carved on fine white marble. The work is carved from a flat slab. The Madonna's face is in profile, and she holds her infant son against her. Considering that Michelangelo was probably only 16 or 17 when this work was done, it shows remarkable talent.

The *Battle of the Centaurs* measures almost twice the size of the *Madonna*. The sculpture is also carved from a slab of marble. It depicts a writhing mass of half-human figures. The piece is unfinished, though; work stopped in 1492 when Lorenzo de Medici died suddenly at the age of 43.

With Lorenzo's death, the artist's paradise at the Medici garden disintegrated. The Medici fortune fell under the rule of Piero de Medici, a relative of Lorenzo. Power and money were Piero's only

concerns. He openly abused his status in Florence. In 1494, after only two years of rule, the Florentines had had enough of Piero. They expelled the bully, who fled north to Bologna, Italy. ❧

The Battle of the Centaurs *is carved in relief, meaning it is carved from a flat slab.*

Chapter
4 A SCULPTOR'S TOUCH

ᥱᎨᏊᏊᎨᏌᏊ

Michelangelo followed Piero de Medici to Bologna. He really had little choice. In those days, when an artist lost a patron, he quickly sought another. It was only through a patron that an artist could afford a decent life. Once in Bologna, though, Michelangelo acquired a new patron—Gianfrancesco Aldovrandi, a nobleman from that city. Michelangelo found work space and began carving.

Other sculptors in Bologna resented Michelangelo's good fortune in finding a financial supporter. They paid rent, bought tools and stone, and survived out of their own pockets. Young Michelangelo, not yet 20 years old, enjoyed a comfortable home, had stone and supplies provided, and received commissions for artworks with little effort. His patron paid for everything.

This painting by French painter Eugene Delacroix shows Michelangelo in his studio surrounded by his work.

Michelangelo soon moved from Aldovrandi to a new patron, Lorenzo di Pierfrancesco de Medici. His new patron encouraged Michelangelo to carve two works, *St. John* and *Sleeping Cupid.* He suggested

Over the course of his career, Michelangelo traveled and worked in much of modern-day Italy.

that Michelangelo try his hand at art fraud. A bit of dirt and false aging would make the *Cupid* more salable in Rome. Lorenzo di Pierfrancesco de Medici advised Michelangelo to bury the piece until it

looked old and then send it to Rome. He said, "I am sure it would pass for an antique, and you would get much more for it than if you sold it here." Michelangelo did as his patron suggested.

Michelangelo went to Rome with letters of introduction from his new patron. He brought his fake antique with him. Cardinal Raffaello Riario purchased the *Sleeping Cupid* and commissioned Michelangelo to produce another, even finer work. Michelangelo wrote to his patron, "The Cardinal asked me whether I was up to making something fine. I answered that ... he would see what I would do. We have bought a piece of marble for a life-size figure, and I shall begin on Monday."

In 1496, Michelangelo carved a figure of Bacchus, the Roman god of wine, from the block of marble the cardinal gave him. Cardinal Riario disliked the sculpture and sold it to a Roman banker, Jacopo Galli.

Michelangelo could not have had better luck. Galli was so impressed with the sculpture that in 1498 he commissioned Michelangelo to carve another piece. This piece was to be a pietà, a traditional depiction of the Virgin Mary holding her dead son. It was planned for display in the Vatican's Virgin Chapel in St. Peter's Basilica. Michelangelo bought a horse and headed to the marble quarries in Carrara, in northern Italy. There, he spent weeks choosing the perfect piece of marble for his statue. He left with a block of exceptionally fine marble, and, under Michelangelo's chisel and hammer, it became an exceptionally fine work of art.

Michelangelo's Pietà *is the first Italian sculpture of the traditional* pietà *subject.*

The *Pietà* features a very young seated and peaceful Virgin. Her face is soft, tender, loving. The

body of her son, Jesus, lies draped across her lap. Her head is bowed and veiled. Only her hands show the sorrow and tension within her.

The *Pietà* caught the eye of many wealthy, powerful men in the Vatican. It led to further commissions, including 15 small statues for Cardinal Francesco Piccolomini. The cardinal wanted a number of statues to decorate the altar of a church in Siena, Italy. However,

> *In the Pietà, the Virgin and her son look to be close to the same age. When criticized about the Virgin's apparent youth, Michelangelo explained that the son had taken on the burdens of mankind and would have aged accordingly.*

another artist had started the project, and Michelangelo disliked finishing someone else's pieces. He completed only four statues before leaving this work undone.

Flitting from one project to another became a bad habit with Michelangelo. He often took on more work than he could complete, and then found himself in legal troubles as he signed and then neglected many contracts. The Piccolomini contract became the first in a string of unfinished works that brought legal consequences.

In 1501, when Michelangelo was 26 years old, Piero Soderini, the Florentine head of government, commissioned Michelangelo to create a large sculpture. Michelangelo gladly stopped work on Cardinal Piccolomini's commission to take on this new

> *As an adult, Michelangelo had broad, powerful shoulders and arms—the result of countless hours working with stone. He had dark hair and brown eyes flecked with gold. He wore his beard divided into two points. His clothes were frequently little more than rags, and they were always covered in marble dust. Nevertheless, he often slept in them. As for meals, a crust of bread and piece of cheese were as fine to Michelangelo as a seven-course dinner. He had little interest in clothing, sleeping, eating, or anything other than his art.*

opportunity. For Michelangelo, there was a tremendous amount of excitement in starting a new project, particularly a large one.

The sculptor left Rome and headed to Florence to work on the stone of a lifetime. Years earlier, a sculptor named Agostino di Duccio had obtained a block of marble so gigantic that few artists would risk working on it. Duccio began the work in Florence and "ruined" the stone. The block lay idle. Several sculptors wanted a chance at the huge stone, but Soderini awarded the commission to Michelangelo.

Once in Florence, Michelangelo immediately surrounded the stone with barricades and began work. Tirelessly, he chipped away at the giant and created *David*. There is some irony in a statue of a biblical giant-killer that is, essentially, of gigantic proportions. His statue of *David* stands 14 feet (4.2 m) tall. It is a nude figure, muscular and young. He carries a sling over one shoulder. David's facial expression shows great determination and intensity.

Michelangelo sketched his ideas for David and other statues before he began carving.

When Soderini saw the *David*, he was delighted. However, when Michelangelo was in the process of putting the final touches on the statue, Soderini commented that David's nose was too thick. Michelangelo realized that Soderini was looking at the head from far below, so he took his chisel and chipped away some marble—not from the nose but from an area that needed smoothing anyway.

Michelangelo's sculpture of David shows the heroic figure before slaying the giant Goliath.

Michelangelo asked Soderini to take another look. Soderini looked at the nose and replied, "It pleases me better. You have given it life."

Soderini paid Michelangelo 400 golden florins for *David*. It would stand in a place of honor in front of the Palazzo Vecchio, the Florentine city hall. To move the massive statue, walls were destroyed and 40 men with rollers pushed the piece through the streets.

Soderini offered Michelangelo a new task. He commissioned Michelangelo, along with painter Leonardo da Vinci, to produce paintings for Florence's Council Hall. Michelangelo chose the war of Pisa as his subject. He drew a rough sketch of the painting, called a cartoon. In the sketch, nude soldiers emerge from bathing in the river Arno. The battle has already started, and they are hurrying from the water to hunt for their weapons and buckle on their arms.

Commissioning two rivals and essentially pitting them against each other should have produced the finest work of each man. Unfortunately, it produced nothing. Leonardo became frustrated with the technicalities of working on that particular painting. Michelangelo left Florence for Rome, as Pope Julius II had summoned Michelangelo to make his tomb. Sculpting was Michelangelo's first love, and he happily left the unfinished painting behind him. ✍

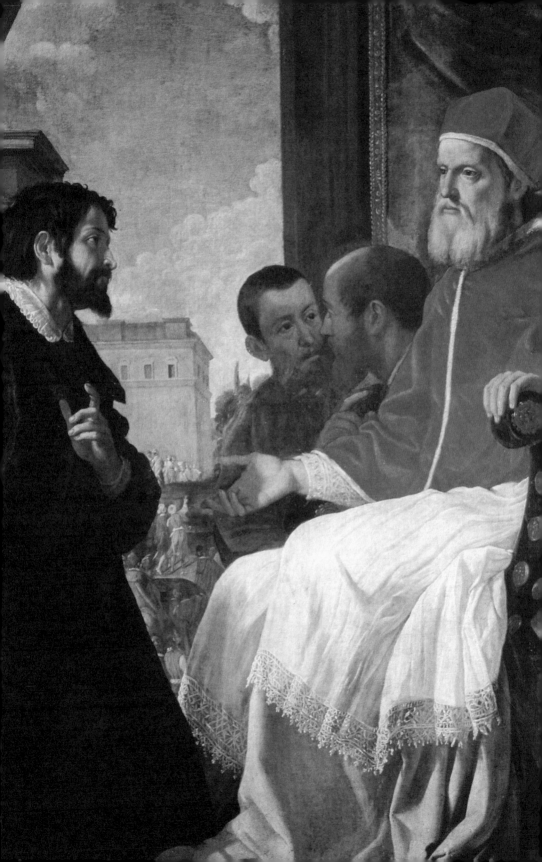

5 A DEMANDING POPE

❧❦❧

Giuliano della Rovere was born to be a pope. His uncle was Pope Sixtus IV, the pope who built the Sistine Chapel. Guiliano himself became a priest at an early age and, in 1471 at 28 years old, he became a cardinal. During the Renaissance, becoming pope was more of a popularity contest than a religious appointment. Power, wealth, and influence made popes. Faith and religious commitment were not major issues. In 1492, Giuliano della Rovere lost the election to pope to a member of the Borgia clan. The Borgias were a powerful Italian family, and Pope Alexander VI openly favored his family ties.

Cardinal della Rovere went to France, where he plotted the assassination of his rival. The plotting came to nothing, and Alexander VI lived for another 11

Michelangelo completed some of his most important works at the request of Pope Julius II (right).

years. Again, della Rovere was passed over in the papal election for Pope Pius III, who served less than a year.

Finally, in 1503, Giuliano got his turn at being pope. As pope, Giuliano chose the name Julius II. Almost immediately upon his election to pope, he summoned Michelangelo, as well as the painter Raphael Sanzio and architect Donato Bramante. He ordered Bramante to rebuild St. Peter's Basilica, the Vatican's main church, Raphael to refurbish and decorate the Vatican apartments, and Michelangelo to create a tomb. Pope Julius had a tremendous ego, and he wanted a tomb to match—a work of monumental proportions. Michelangelo designed a memorial 34 feet (10.4 m) by 50 feet (15.2 m). The entire tomb was to feature arches, columns, medallions, and statues. Michelangelo would personally carve 40 life-size marble statues, including one of Pope Julius II and one of Moses with the Ten Commandments. For this effort,

Pope Julius commissioned painter Raphael Sanzio to refurbish and decorate the Vatican apartments.

Michelangelo was to receive a salary of 1,200 ducats yearly. At that time, this sum equaled the combined wages of 10 average craftsmen for one year.

Michelangelo immediately headed north to Carrara again to choose his marble. A tomb of such a size required several tons of fine stone. Some needed to match in color, others had to stand out. Michelangelo had no idea that the pope's interests quickly flitted from one project to another. Out of sight, for this pope, meant out of mind and onto the next project. Michelangelo was gone for eight months buying stone. When he returned, the tomb had been put on hold due to lack of money. The pope's interests now concentrated on rebuilding St. Peter's Basilica.

Architect Donato Bramante was commissioned to rebuild the Vatican's St. Peter's Basilica.

The basilica was a builder's nightmare. The original builders erected the church on a swamp. Rumors flowed about the cellars being alive with snakes. The foundation was so poorly laid that the building had a slight tilt. Michelangelo returned to Rome to find a new foundation being dug. Stones and building equipment filled the Vatican's streets and plazas. The new basilica needed tons of stone and thousands of workers, all of which required plenty of gold coin. Funds for the tomb would have to come later.

Irritated, Michelangelo returned to Florence. If the pope chose to ignore him, Michelangelo would do likewise. In 1506, Michelangelo wrote a lengthy let-

Pope Julius II, shown here, made so many demands that Michelangelo often felt he was a slave to Julius's whims.

ter to Giuliano da Sangallo, an architect working with Bramante:

> *I learned from one of yours [letters] how the Pope took my departure badly, and how His Holiness is going to make a deposit [of gold] and do what he had agreed, and that I should come back and not be doubtful about anything... His Holiness should know that I am more disposed than ever to go on with this work, and if he wants the tomb built no matter what, it shouldn't bother him where I build it, so long as at the end of the five years that we agreed on it is put up in St. Peter's.*

Michelangelo returned to Rome and set up his workshop again. The pope visited him in his house, admired Michelangelo's work, and gave the artist his blessing. Content that he was in Pope Julius's good graces, Michelangelo continued planning the massive memorial. However, Julius now had another project in mind. ℘

L I B I C A

Chapter 6 THE SISTINE CHAPEL

∽◦∽

Few tasks could be more depressing than for a sculptor to be forced to paint. At least, this was Michelangelo's opinion of the new project set for him by Pope Julius II. He must have gazed up at the Sistine Chapel's blue ceiling and gold stars and grit his teeth in disgust. Like many people faced with unpleasant tasks, he considered himself something of a slave to Pope Julius's whims. Michelangelo wrote, "This is not my profession. I am wasting my time, and all for nothing. May God help me!"

The chapel's ceiling covered a curved surface of about 5,600 square feet (507 square meters). Besides being curved, the ceiling had an uneven surface. The size was irregular, wider toward the back of the chapel than at the altar. Added to the obvious problems

In the arched shapes that surrounded the edges of the ceiling, Michelangeo painted sibyls, female prophets from ancient Greece and Rome.

was the ceiling's immense height—60 feet (18 m) above the chapel floor. To this odd surface, Michelangelo was to paint scenes from the Old Testament.

Michelangelo's basic plan included nine scenes from the book of Genesis. He decided to present the separation of light from dark, the creation of the sun, moon, and planets, and the division of land and

The Sistine Chapel is part of the Vatican complex in Rome, Italy.

water. Next, he would depict the creation of Adam, the making of Eve, and the temptation and expulsion of Adam and Eve from paradise. The last three scenes would include the sacrifice of Noah, the Great Flood, and Noah's drunkenness. Each scene had to be far larger than life. The art would be viewed from 60 feet (18 m) away. For the scenes to be fully appreciated, they needed to be supersized.

Around the edges of the ceiling, Michelangelo planned to paint architectural borders or dividers. These divisions broke the ceiling into arched shapes. Within the arched divisions, Michelangelo planned portraits of the great prophets of the Old Testament, such as Jonah, Daniel, Jeremiah, Ezekiel, Joel, and Isaiah. Alternating with the prophets would be sibyls, female prophets of ancient Greece and Rome.

That might seem like plenty of art to fill the ceiling, but it was not enough. Four biblical scenes would grace the corners. They would depict David and Goliath, Judith and the beheading of Holofernes, the Brazen Serpent, and the crucifixion of Haman. In the remaining space, ancestors of Jesus would appear, such as Boaz, David, Jesse, Solomon, Jacob, and Joseph. In all, the ceiling would incorporate 300 human figures.

Michelangelo's task might have been easier if he had paid attention to his lessons as Ghirlandaio's apprentice. But that was when he was a child, and no one could tell him what to do. So now he faced a massive task made more difficult by his lack of knowledge about fresco painting.

Fresco painting was more difficult than painting oil on canvas or wood. First, the surface was prepared with a rough, coarse layer of plaster. When the rough plaster dried, the painter added a thin, smoother layer of plaster. At this point, the drawing, called a cartoon, was traced onto the damp plaster. Colors were mixed and painting began while the plaster was still damp. The paint was absorbed and became part of the plaster.

In April 1508, Michelangelo hired several assistants from Florence. These assistants helped with preparing the ceiling, but did not paint much. Stubbornness prevented Michelangelo from asking known fresco artists to help. Instead, he worked by trial and error, finally attaining the process and techniques of fresco painting.

A month later, Michelangelo received his contract for the ceil-

> *The word* fresco *comes from an Italian word meaning "fresh." This type of painting requires freshly laid plaster, and an artist lays only as much plaster as can be painted in a day. Fresco painting reached its height during the Italian Renaissance of the 1400s and 1500s, but Mexican artists, Diego Rivera and Jose Clemente Orozco, helped revive fresco painting in the United States in the 1930s.*

In one of the main panels of the ceiling, Michelangelo painted Adam and Eve being expelled from paradise.

ing and a healthy 500 ducats on account. He hired a professional mason to lay the rough plaster layer. While this was done, the assistants erected a scaffold from which to work. Of course, Pope Julius did not intend to lose the use of his chapel during the painting process. Work began on one section while Mass proceeded below. No plaster, paint, or tools could drop to the chapel floor. They might strike a cardinal, bishop, or even the pope himself.

The painting consisted of three separate periods. The first began in September 1508 but was halted due to mold in the plaster. An engineer had to be hired to rid the chapel of excess moisture, thus allowing the plaster and paint to dry properly.

The second period ran through the fall of 1510. Despite the heavy demands of work, Michelangelo managed to keep in close contact with his father and brothers in Florence. Whenever he lived away from home, he wrote regularly and vented his irritations through letters. Michelangelo, an avid complainer, wrote to his brother Buonarroto to tell him of his

In this letter, written in 1509, Michelangelo complains to his father about his lack of funds.

woes: "I live here in great toil and great weariness of body, and have no friends of any kind and don't want any and haven't the time to eat what I need."

The painting itself proved difficult. Some of the work could be done in a standing position, painting on the wall directly in front of him. As the ceiling curved above, however, the painting had to be done overhead with the arm extended. Hours of painting in this position strained even the strongest arm and back muscles. In addition, Pope Julius constantly pressured Michelangelo to finish the work.

The pope was forever asking him when the painting would be done. Michelangelo answered, "It will be finished when I have satisfied myself."

Said Pope Julius, "But we will that you would satisfy us in our desire to have it done quickly." Under his breath, he added that he would have Michelangelo thrown from the scaffolding if the painting was not soon completed.

Michelangelo wrote a sonnet describing his experience painting the ceiling:

> *A goiter it seems I got from this backward cran-*
> *ing like the cats get there in Lombardy, or wherever—*
> *bad water, they say, from lapping their fetid river.*
> *My belly, tugged under my chin, 's all out of*
> *whack. Beard points like a finger at heaven. Near*
> *the back of my neck, skull scrapes where a hunch-*
> *back's lump would be.*

I'm pigeon-breasted, a harpy! Face dribbled—
see?—like a Byzantine floor, mosaic. From
all this straining my guts and my hambones
tangle, pretty near.

Thank God I can swivel my butt about for
ballast. Feet are out of sight; they just scuffle
around, erratic.

Up front my hide's tight elastic; in the rear
it's slack and droopy, except where crimps
have callused. I'm bent like a bow, half-round,
type Asiatic.

Not odd that what's on my mind,
when expressed, comes out weird, jumbled.
Don't berate; no gun with its barrel screwy can
shoot straight.

Giovanni, come agitate for my pride, my
poor dead art! I don't belong! Who's a painter?
Me? No way! They've got me wrong.

Michelangelo's talent
defined his personality.
He had a large,
uncontrolled ego
and often felt rejected
by others, claiming
their behavior was
due to jealousy of his
talent. He also had
a troubled relationship
with his father, whose
disapproval he had
risked in order to
become an artist.

Michelangelo continued to moan over his workload and his money situation. The financial woes must be looked at with some disbelief. While he regularly complained of being treated badly, paid poorly, and forced to live in poverty, Michelangelo also supported his father, brothers, and their families. He helped them set up businesses, buy farms, and purchase needed goods. For a poor artist,

Michelangelo always seemed to have enough money for his family's needs.

Between the fall of 1510 and summer of 1511, Michelangelo stopped painting. He wanted money, and his funds had dried up. He explained his situation to his father in a letter dated September 5, 1510:

This portrait of Michelangelo was painted by his contemporary, Guiliano Bugiardini.

> *I am still to receive 500 ducats through the agreement, which I have earned, and the pope was to give me another equal amount to start the other part of the work. And he has left here and left no order for me, so that I find myself without money and don't know what I am to do.*

At this point, about half the ceiling had been finished. The scaffolding came down, and Michelangelo could appraise his work. What he discovered caused a major adjustment in the remaining painting. He had begun at one end on Noah's scenes, and they were too small. Michelangelo immediately began preparing for the next section, with even larger portrayals of God, Adam, and Eve.

The third and final stage of painting began in the summer of 1511, when Pope Julius arranged for Michelangelo's money. For several years, Florence had been in turmoil with the threat of Spanish invasion and a serious lack of Florentine leadership. The Medici family returned to power, and political life in Florence smoothed out.

As the Sistine Chapel neared completion, Michelangelo again complained about his lack of funds. In a letter dated September 18, 1512, Michelangelo tells his brother Buonarroto,

> *I can tell you that I haven't a farthing and I'm barefoot and naked, one might say, and I can't get my balance until I have finished the work, and I suffer the greatest toil and discomfort.*

Pope Julius was delighted with the results, although he had a few suggestions for changes. He wanted the figures painted with more gold and, perhaps, richer clothing. Michelangelo refused. He said, "In those times men did not wear gold, and those whom I am painting were never very rich, but holy men despising riches." This may have been the only argument Michelangelo won in dealing with Pope Julius. Michelangelo was less thrilled with the results. He complained that "this work was not as complete as I should have liked; the pope's haste prevented my finishing it."

On November 1, 1512, All Saints' Day, Pope Julius opened his finished Sistine Chapel for Mass. Cardinals, bishops, priests, nuns, and Roman nobility filed into the chapel. When the Mass began, all eyes should have been on the altar, but they were not. They rose to the ceiling above.

There, scene after scene stretched out before them. They saw God reclining between the darkness and the light. His hands extended to the sun on one side, the moon on the other. Life poured from God's

The Creation of Adam *is one of the main panels of the Sistine Chapel ceiling fresco.*

The Sistine Chapel's ceiling frescoes cover over 5,600 square feet (507 square meters).

index finger into the reclining figure of Adam. Eve, a full-grown woman, rose from Adam's body. A wily snake curled around a tree, tempting Adam and Eve into sin.

A flood swept across one scene, with Noah surviving and all other souls lost. Prophets and sibyls burst from their painted marble seats. They seemed to be leaning forward, engaging the viewers below. Bible stories came to life, as David slew Goliath and Haman died on a cross. For a man who hated painting, Michelangelo surpassed even his own modest expectations. The ceiling frescoes of the Vatican's Sistine Chapel have awed viewers for centuries.

In addition to sibyls, prophets, and figures from the book of Genesis, Michelangelo also painted other, smaller figures throughout the ceiling fresco. Among them are cherubs and seated male nudes, or ignudi, which are modeled after classical Greek sculpture and show the human form at its most idealized.

7 TOMBS AND TROUBLES

෴

The Julius tomb became an on-again, off-again project covering nearly 40 years. In 1513, need for a completed tomb increased. Pope Julius had died and requested in his will that his family make sure the tomb was finished.

Michelangelo had already collected several thousand ducats for his work. He had spent hundreds of ducats purchasing and moving marble. Again, money became an issue. Pope Julius's family wanted to fulfill his last request. However, they did not want to go broke in order to do so.

Updated plans scaled down the memorial from a freestanding monument to a decorative wall. The new sketch reduced the number of statues and lowered the cost. The seated Moses remained as the

Many consider the statue of Moses from the tomb of Pope Julius II to be one of Michelangelo's finest works.

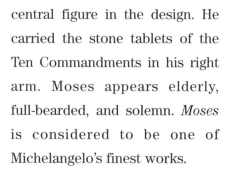

central figure in the design. He carried the stone tablets of the Ten Commandments in his right arm. Moses appears elderly, full-bearded, and solemn. *Moses* is considered to be one of Michelangelo's finest works.

The tomb's lower level featured several figures of captives. The captives represented the common man. These figures included the *Bound Captive* and the *Dying Captive*. These two statues are no longer part of the tomb, but are on display in the Louvre Museum in Paris, France. The statues seem only partially finished. This was typical of Michelangelo's sculpting style. He believed that, as he worked, figures emerged from the marble. His job was not to carve a statue, but to release forms from within the living stone.

For three years, Michelangelo worked almost exclusively on the tomb. But times and popes changed, and finishing the tomb would wait many years.

Upon the death of Pope Julius, the church had chosen Pope Leo X as the new pope. Leo X began life as Giovanni de Medici, son of Lorenzo the

Magnificent and a childhood friend of Michelangelo. Giovanni's career in the church was somewhat odd. He became a cardinal at age 14. He was elected pope in 1513, at age 38. It was only after he became pope that Giovanni took holy orders and became a priest.

The Dying Captive *from* Pope Julius II's *tomb is now* at the Louvre Museum in Paris, France.

Giovanni changed his name to Leo X, but he did not change his ways. As a child, Pope Leo X had been spoiled and indulged. He continued on this path as an adult. So, while Michelangelo chipped away at the Julius tomb, Leo X seethed with envy. He wanted Michelangelo to work on a project for him, not for the former pope. And so, Leo X came up with a plan.

In 1517, the pope asked Michelangelo to design a new facade for the church of San Lorenzo in Florence. Michelangelo had little experience with architecture, yet he was confident that he could produce a fine design. Once a contract had been signed, Michelangelo headed north to Carrara to choose the stones. Of course, experience should have warned Michelangelo that popes did not always fulfill their side of a contract.

Once he arrived in Carrara, the question arose as to whether the project would proceed as planned. The sculptor wrote to Rome in May 1517,

> *I feel capable of doing this work, the facade of San Lorenzo, so that it can be the mirror of all Italy in architecture and sculpture, but the Pope [Leo X] and the Cardinal must decide quickly whether they want me to do it or not. ... I have ordered many blocks of marble...and given money here and there, and had digging started in many places... If I knew I*

had to arrange labor and price, I wouldn't worry about throwing in four hundred ducats...and I would take three or four of the best men there and assign all the marbles to them...

Michelangelo sketched his plans for the facade of the church of San Lorenzo in Florence, Italy.

The cost of the facade, in the style in which I propose to have it done and get it underway, including everything so that the Pope would not have to bother about anything afterwards, cannot be less than thirty-five thousand gold ducats...and for this I would undertake to do it in six years...

Even the self-indulgent Pope Leo X could not pay this amount without flinching. However, keeping Michelangelo away from work on the Julius tomb was a worthy cause. And so, Michelangelo continued to choose marble, pay out cash, and plan the facade.

In 1520, Michelangelo's two main projects—the Julius tomb and the San Lorenzo facade—were both only partially completed. The progress on the Julius tomb had slowed to a snail's pace, and Michelangelo needed a place to work on the facade. He purchased a piece of land near the church to set up his workshop. Not too surprisingly, shortly thereafter the San Lorenzo facade was placed on hold and then cancelled altogether.

This distressed Michelangelo greatly. He wrote at length about

Although both the Julius tomb and the facade of San Lorenzo required architectural planning, Michelangelo probably had no formal training as an architect. During the Renaissance period, however, artists were often given such commissions simply based on their ability to draw and create designs.

Although Michelangelo presented Pope Leo X with his plans for the facade of San Lorenzo, his designs were never put in place.

the costs, both financial and physical, of working on the San Lorenzo facade. He had bought stone, made wax models, hired people to work, and purchased land. Michelangelo said,

> *I am not charging to the pope's account the*
> *fact that I have been ruined over said work*
> *at San Lorenzo: I am not charging to his*
> *account the enormous insult of having*
> *been brought here to execute the said work*
> *and then having it taken away from me...*

Michelangelo continually recounted the many insults he endured.

In place of the facade, Michelangelo received a different project, the Medici tombs. Two young Medici men died at an early age. Young Giuliano, Duke de Nemours, died in 1516, at 38 years old. The second young Medici, Lorenzo de Medici, Duke of Urbino, died in 1519, at 27 years of age.

Leo X and other members of the Medici family decided to erect a tomb in honor of their deceased relatives. Plans for the Medici tombs progressed. Michelangelo designed two opposite scenarios for Lorenzo and Giuliano. Lorenzo would appear quiet, thoughtful, and serious. Statues of *Dawn and Dusk* would grace

Michelangelo created the two Medici tombs as large wall structures to be placed across from one another. In addition to the tombs, he designed the Medici Chapel, in which the tombs are placed. This chapel is part of San Lorenzo, and like the facade of the church itself, Michelangelo's work on the chapel was not completed.

The tomb of Lorenzo de Medici, Duke of Urbino, features reclining statues that depict Dawn and Dusk.

his tomb. Giuliano would appear active, outgoing, and lively. His tomb would have the parallel statues of *Day and Night.*

Throughout this time, Michelangelo continued to hope that he would be able to resume work on the San Lorenzo facade. Then, Leo X died in 1521. The San Lorenzo facade project—and Michelangelo's hopes—died with him.

Two years later, in 1523, another Medici rose to become pope. This was Giuliano de Medici, Lorenzo the Magnificent's nephew and another childhood friend of Michelangelo's. Giuliano took as his name Pope Clement VII. This Medici pope wanted two things from Michelangelo. First, Michelangelo was to finish Pope Julius's tomb. Second, he was to complete the Medici tombs at San Lorenzo.

Clement VII knew that Michelangelo was inclined to take on too much new work. He told Michelangelo, "If someone asks you for a painting, attach a brush to your foot, make four strokes with it and tell them, 'The painting is finished.'"

Some historians paint a picture of an agonized, friendless Michelangelo sculpting alone in some dark workshop. Nothing could be farther from the truth. Between 1516 and 1534, the "tombs period," Michelangelo hired some 300 various workers to assist on his projects.

He personally selected his workforce of friends, associates, and trained professionals, and knew them all by name. He gave most of them colorful nicknames, such as the Stick, the Basket, the Little Liar, the Dolt, Oddball, Fats, Thorny, Lefty, Stumpy, and Gloomy.

Michelangelo also maintained several long-term friendships, but he held quite low opinions of many of these men. He regularly accused them of lying, cheating, and theft. He called them wretches, scoundrels, swindlers, and criminals. Clearly, being Michelangelo's friend required serious effort.

Although Michelangelo handpicked his staff, he often thought little of those with whom he worked.

As the artist aged, he brooded and complained more. His temperament became more explosive,

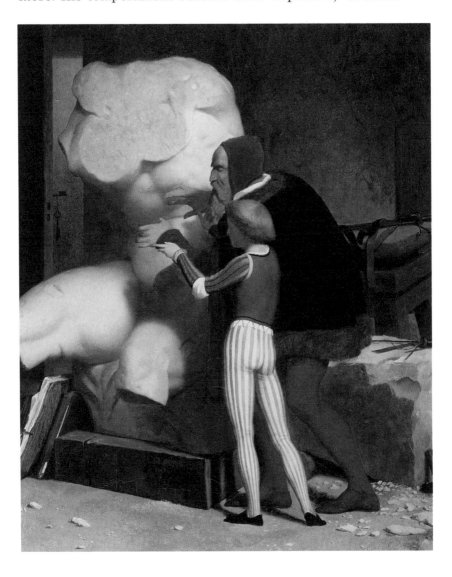

and he easily took offense. His commitment to his work increased, and he continued to take on more work than he could complete.

During the 1520s, Florence fell on hard times. The city needed to defend itself against invasion. Florence was a small, independent republic at that

Michelangelo sketched plans to fortify a gate in Florence.

time. It did not have the power of an Italian army to fend off invaders. And so, Michelangelo offered his services for another task: governor and procurator general for the defense of Florence. This grand title, simplified, meant that he was to build protective walls around the city. Michelangelo, sculptor and painter, became Michelangelo, military engineer. He took on this job with the same zeal and energy that he had shown for other tasks. Of course, this meant slighting Pope Clement VII and the tomb projects still in production.

While in Florence, Michelangelo continued to sculpt. He hammered away at the Medici tomb figures and two works that he would never finish, *Victory* and the *Medici Madonna*.

Michelangelo remained in Florence until 1534, when major events took place that changed the remaining years of his life. Pope Clement VII died and was replaced by Alessandro Farnese, Pope Paul III. Michelangelo went back to Rome, never to return to Florence. The Medici tombs and the Julius II tomb remained unfinished. Work on them continued from Rome. ❧

8

THE LAST FLICKERS OF GREATNESS

❧⌘❧

A new pope brought, as usual, new projects for Michelangelo. Pope Paul III belonged to a noble family. He was not a Medici, but had been connected to Lorenzo the Magnificent's court. In his mid-60s when he became pope, he was elderly by Renaissance standards. Wild in his youth, Paul III mellowed in his old age. He reformed the Catholic Church and rewarded the efforts of deserving clergy rather than relatives.

Like Julius II, Pope Paul III wanted to redecorate the Sistine Chapel. He asked Michelangelo to paint a fresco on the altar wall. Michelangelo tried to refuse, but the pope did not listen. Michelangelo reminded the pope that he had to finish the Julius tomb. Pope Julius's family had taken legal action against

Michelangelo spent five years painting The Last Judgment *on the altar wall in the Sistine Chapel.*

Michelangelo: either finish the tomb or return the money paid in advance.

Pope Paul shouted, "I have nursed this ambition for 30 years, and now that I'm pope, am I not to have it satisfied? I shall tear the [Julius tomb] contract up. I'm determined to have you in my service, no matter what." Thus, Michelangelo found himself gritting his teeth once again and painting another huge fresco.

The Last Judgment, begun in 1536, bears a somber, almost depressing mood. The overall size of the fresco, although not as large as the Sistine Chapel ceiling, measures 48 feet (14.5 m) by 43 feet (13 m). The theme is the final judgment at the end of the world. The picture features hundreds of figures, all painted in the nude. Jesus Christ, a clap of thunder in his hand, fills the center. To the left, souls rise toward heaven. Their faces mirror their joy, triumph, and peace at earning God's reward. To the right, souls drift downward toward hell. Their looks present terror, despair, and sorrow.

Michelangelo spent five years, from age 61 to 66, painting *The Last Judgment*. The painting represents his own despair as his life was, he believed, coming to an end. He had already outlived the normal life span of the time by roughly 20 years. Michelangelo's own image appears on the painting in the depiction of the flayed skin of Saint Bartholomew. He was a martyr who had been skinned alive for his faith.

Many called *The Last Judgment* shameful. Biagio da Cesena, the Vatican's master of ceremonies, said,

It was mostly disgraceful that in so sacred a place there should have been

In this detail from The Last Judgment, *the face on the flayed skin of martyr Saint Bartholomew is painted to resemble Michelangelo himself.*

depicted all those nude figures, exposing
themselves so shamefully, and that it was
no work for a papal chapel but rather for
the public baths and taverns.

Later, the church hired an artist to cover the figures in discreet places. From that time on, the artist
was known as the "breeches-maker,"—the
painter who put pants on Michelangelo's great art.
The recent restoration of the Sistine Chapel frescoes
removed some of the added draperies.

While painting *The Last Judgment*, Michelangelo
became close friends with the noblewoman Vittoria
Colonna. Vittoria lost her husband at a fairly young
age, and she chose to remain a widow for the rest of
her life. For nearly a dozen years, the two were close
friends. Michelangelo had been scribbling short poems
in the margins of his sketches—a
kind of reverse doodling. Vittoria
took Michelangelo's poetry seri-
ously. She encouraged him to pursue his writing.

It was during this period that
Michelangelo accepted a major
architectural project: the design
of the Capitoline Hill. The site
had a grisly history, having been
used for executing criminals and
political enemies during the

> *Michelangelo wrote*
> *some of his finest*
> *poems for Vittoria*
> *Colonna, who was*
> *herself a poet. In*
> *addition, he made*
> *several drawings for*
> *and of her, and several*
> *of his images of Mary*
> *are believed to be based*
> *on her appearance.*

Michelangelo sketched this portrait of a woman who may be his friend Vittoria Colonna.

Middle Ages. By the early 1500s, the Capitoline area had evolved into something of a slum. The hill overlooked the Roman Forum, yet few visitors could trek through the muck to enjoy the view.

In 1538, Michelangelo began designing a spacious public square, an elegant stairway, and facades for buildings around the plaza. Today, tourists climb Michelangelo's gently rising ramp

Michelangelo's plans for the Capitoline Hill were completed after his death.

from the streets below to the hilltop. There, they find a broad plaza featuring a statue of Marcus Aurelius. The plaza itself is laid out in a starburst pattern. Surrounding the plaza are the Senate, the

Conservatori, and the Braccio Nuovo. Broad, sweeping staircases line either side of the entrance to the Senate. Although the design had been sketched in 1538, the actual work was not completed until well after Michelangelo's death. He never saw the finished results of one of his finest architectural designs.

In 1541, Pope Paul III had Michelangelo's next commission ready. Earlier, the pope had ordered a new chapel built to serve as his private place of worship. Called the Pauline Chapel, it was finished in 1540, with bare walls just waiting for a new set of Michelangelo frescoes.

The artist chose as his subjects the conversion of St. Paul and the crucifixion of St. Peter. These subjects depicted serious themes. *The Conversion of Saint Paul* features an angry God who sends a light so bright that Paul must shut his eyes against the brilliance. God is surrounded by a host of angels, while Paul lies among men, all shying away from God's light. *The Crucifixion of St. Peter* features a humble Peter being hung upside down on a cross. A crowd surrounds the dying saint during his last moments of life.

With the completion of these two frescoes, Michelangelo no doubt breathed a sigh of relief. He would not paint again. Though he had created many magnificent frescoes, Michelangelo still believed that painting was a false art. He wrote,

The more painting resembles sculpture, the better I like it, and the more sculpture resembles painting, the worse I like it. Sculpture is the torch by which painting is illuminated, and the difference between them is the difference between the sun and the moon.

Finally, Michelangelo had time to complete Julius II's tomb. The final version featured the Moses figure with statues of Rachel and Leah on either side. The tomb was installed in 1545 in the church of San Pietro in Vincoli, in Rome. Michelangelo had closed out a contract originally written more than 40 years earlier.

Now, Michelangelo's eyes turned again toward architecture. He had devoted much of his adult life to serving various popes, and this would not change. In 1546, Pope Paul III asked Michelangelo to complete the unfinished work of Bramante and Sangallo—St. Peter's Basilica.

Michelangelo thought that St. Peter's might be the last and greatest of his achievements. He wrote to his nephew Lionardo, "Many believe, —and I believe— that I have been designated for this work by God. In spite of my old age, I do not want to give it up; I work out of love for God and I put all my hope in Him."

Work on St. Peter's was never pleasant. Too many political groups made for very slow progress

on the great church. Factions within the church chose their favorites and supported their actions. When Pope Paul III selected Michelangelo to head the work, those factions became hostile.

After many years of interrupted work, Michelangelo finally finished Julius's tomb.

Michelangelo designed the dome on St. Peter's Basilica.

As architect, Michelangelo hoped to create a final plan that would block changes once he died. He designed, as the focal point of the church, a brilliant dome. So fine is the architectural plan of Michelangelo's dome that it has been copied many times throughout the world. The dome on the United States Capitol building is inspired by Michelangelo's St. Peter's dome.

After about a dozen years of close friendship, Vittoria died in 1547. Her loss overwhelmed Michelangelo. Already weary, he became more sullen and depressed. He wrote these lines of poetry in her memory:

> *When the prime mover of many sighs*
> *Heaven took through death from out her*
> *earthly place*
> *Nature, that never made so fair a face,*
> *Remained ashamed, and tears were in*
> *all eyes.*

Stone now consumed Michelangelo's talents. No matter what project he worked on, he spent part of every day with hammer and chisel in hand. His energetic work style continued with the same power he showed early in life. A friend observed,

> *I have seen Michelangelo, although more*
> *than sixty years old and no longer among*
> *the most robust, knock off more chips of a*
> *very hard marble in a quarter of an hour*
> *than three young stone carvers could have*
> *done in three or four [hours], an almost*
> *incredible thing to one who had not seen it.*

About this time Michelangelo began working on a new statue—one he planned for his own tomb.

Called the Florentine *Pietà*, the statue stood 7.5 feet (2.3 m) tall. The four-figure group features the dead Jesus Christ in the forefront. To the side, kneels the Virgin Mary with her hand supporting the body of her son. Nicodemus, hooded and somber, stands directly behind the Christ figure.

Michelangelo carved the figure of Nicodemus in his Florentine Pietà *in his own image.*

The Florentine *Pietà* is oddly carved. The Christ figure is missing a leg, although most viewers rarely notice the loss. The Virgin's figure remains unfinished, as does much of the piece.

Michelangelo worked on this piece occasionally for eight years. Old and tired, he poured his depression over his life into the statue. The work went poorly. Fed up with the results, Michelangelo took his chisel to the statue and destroyed it. A young sculptor and friend, Tiberio Calcagni, asked Michelangelo if he could finish the *Pietà*. With the artist's approval, Calcagni repaired and polished parts of the statue. He added little to the design out of respect for Michelangelo's talent. Today, the statue stands on display in the Museo Dell Opera Del Duomo in Florence.

Regardless of Michelangelo's advanced age and growing depression, the pope's work had to continue. As with several other popes before him, Paul III did not survive to see his projects fulfilled. He died in 1549 and was followed by Pope Julius III, born Giovanni Maria del Monte. The new Pope Julius was a large, gruff, stingy man. Like many of the previous popes, Julius III strongly favored Michelangelo. The pair appeared comfortable with each other, openly chatting about architecture. Julius III openly defended the artist against the politics involved in building St. Peter's Basilica.

While the endless backbiting continued at St. Peter's, Michelangelo chipped away with hammer and chisel in his workshop. After destroying the Florentine *Pietà*, he began a new piece in 1556, the Rondanini *Pietà*. The statue is the roughest hewn of

The Rondanini Pietà *is more roughly carved than most of Michelangelo's other works.*

Michelangelo's pietàs. The Virgin stands behind the Christ figure. Both appear gaunt, coarse, and sorrowful. The mother caresses her son but provides little support for his body.

The Florentine and Rondanini Pietàs are unusual among Michelangelo's works in that he created them for his own satisfaction and not at the request of a patron.

Death drifted in waves through Michelangelo's life. Since few men of his era lived to age 50, he saw friends and family die before him. He outlived the nine popes for whom he worked. He lost his faithful servant, Urbino, which may have had a greater effect on him than any other loss. They had been close companions for 25 years when Urbino died. True to their friendship, Michelangelo provided for the care of Urbino's widow.

By 1563, the artist was simply worn out. He barely slept, working at night by candlelight. After years of letters to his brothers and nephews, he found he could no longer write easily. His secretary wrote, and Michelangelo signed. His eagerness to meet his death is shown in his poem "On the Brink of Death," which begins,

> *Now hath my life across a stormy sea*
> *Like a frail bark reached that wide port where all*
> *Are bidden, ere the final reckoning fall*
> *Of good and evil for eternity...*
> *And ends...*

Painting nor sculpture now can lull to rest
My soul that turns to His great love on high,
Whose arms to clasp us on the cross were spread.

Michelangelo's tomb is in the Santa Croce Church in Florence, Italy.

In February 1564, Michelangelo chiseled away at the Rondanini *Pietà* although he felt chilled and

feverish. For some unknown reason, he chose to burn many of his earlier sketches while weak with fever.

Michelangelo died February 18, 1564, a few weeks shy of his 90th birthday. According to Michelangelo's biographer, Giorgio Vasari, the artist made a short, three-sentence will. He died with his friends Tommaso Cavalieri and Daniele da Volterra by his side. Michelangelo left "his soul to God, his body to the earth, and his material possessions to his nearest relations."

He left very little behind. The unfinished Rondanini *Pietà* survived as his final work. At Michelangelo's request, his body was laid to rest in Santa Croce Church in Florence.

Art historians consider Michelangelo one of the greatest artists of all time. His statues of *David*, the *Pietà*, and *Moses* pulse with life. Although he claimed never to be a painter, his Sistine Chapel ceiling and *The Last Judgment* frescoes draw the admiration of millions. As for architecture, St. Peter's Basilica and the Capitoline Hill stand as reminders of his greatness. Given a choice, Michelangelo would probably have preferred to be remembered the way he often signed his letters: Michelangelo, sculptor. ❧

9 INCHES AT A TIME

❧⊱✦⊰❧

Sweat poured off the brow of Gianluigi Colalucci. As a professional restorer, he had cleaned many valuable works of art in the past. But this was different. This was not simple oil paint on canvas. These were some of the world's greatest art treasures: the Vatican's Sistine Chapel frescoes. The frescoes represented the finest work of renowned Renaissance artists—Botticelli, Ghirlandaio, Perugino, and Michelangelo.

Colalucci gently applied a cleaning solution to a tiny section of a fresco barely larger than his thumbprint. Colalucci's job meant washing away the filth without damaging the art. With painstaking care, he wiped off 500 years of soot and grime.

In 1980, the effort to clean the Sistine Chapel's walls began in earnest. No one knew what the restorers

Gianluigi Colalucci restores a fresco in the Vatican's Sistine Chapel.

would find under the layers of grit, candle soot, pollution, oil, grease, and varnish. The original colors were covered with this dirt, making the original yellows, blues, reds, and greens the Renaissance artists had painted appear brown, black, and gray.

Work progressed inches at a time. The restorers knew that hurrying might destroy irreplaceable art treasures.

The restoration blended careful handiwork with modern technology. Computers analyzed the varnishes coating the chapel's ceiling and walls. X-rays revealed the original look of the paintings. Many nudes had been "dressed" by painting loincloths or draped fabric over body parts. In some cases, the added clothing came off with the dirt. Another computer mapped every curve and crack in the walls and ceilings. Saving the frescoes required fixing damaged or weak plaster without damaging the pictures.

Most traditional cleaning products were considered too harsh for the delicate plaster, and some restorers claimed even water was potentially damaging to the art. Restorers used

In the 18th and 19th centuries, cleaning works of art walked a fine line between restoration and destruction. In those times, art was often cleaned by coating the surface of the painting with oil and then setting the oil on fire. Once the fire had dissolved the dirt, the flames were extinguished— hopefully without damaging the art.

technology such as lasers, electron beams, and even bacteria to clean the frescoes.

Restorers use computers to analyze the materials that coat the Sistine Chapel frescoes.

Cardinal Edmund Szoka, the Vatican's governor, said, "This restoration and the expertise of the restorers allows us to contemplate the paintings as if we had been given the chance of being present when they were first shown."

Not everyone agreed with Cardinal Szoka. Many art historians raged over what they saw as destroying great art. Some feared the restored frescoes didn't show the correct colors. The cleaner version

Restoration revealed the true colors of the Sistine Chapel's frescoes.

of Michelangelo's ceiling burst with bright yellows, vivid greens, soft rose-hued skin, and brilliant blues. The brilliance of Michelangelo's colors astounded art critics and historians. Some critics thought the restorers changed the colors. They never imagined that Michelangelo's original colors from 500 years ago were so bright and lively.

The ceiling restoration took 13 years—twice as long as it took Michelangelo to paint it to begin with. Cleaning all the chapel's art took nearly 20 years. The Vatican had special air filters installed to block out pollution from Rome's air and the breath of millions of visitors.

In December 1999, Pope John Paul II reopened the Sistine Chapel. He said, "These works of art continue to vibrate with mystery in a language that will never grow old." ❧

Life and Times

MICHELANGELO'S LIFE

1475

Michelangelo is born
March 6, 1475, in
Caprese, Italy

1481

Michelangelo's
mother dies

1488

Michelangelo is
apprenticed to the
painter Ghirlandaio

1475

1485

1485

Henry VII is crowned
King of England,
beginning the
117-year reign of
England's Tudor
dynasty

WORLD EVENTS

1490

Lorenzo de Medici becomes Michelangelo's patron

1496

Michelangelo departs for Rome

1498

Work begins on the *Pietà* for St. Peter's in Rome

1495

1492

Ferdinand and Isabella of Spain finance the voyage of the Italian Christopher Columbus to the New World

1497

Vasco da Gama becomes the first western European to find a sea route to India

MICHELANGELO'S LIFE

1504

The statue of *David* is unveiled

1505

Pope Julius II asks Michelangelo to design his tomb

1501

Michelangelo receives a commission to create a sculpture of *David*

1500

1503

Italian artist Leonardo da Vinci begins painting the *Mona Lisa*

1502

Montezuma II becomes ruler of Mexico's Aztec empire

WORLD EVENTS

1512

Michelangelo finishes the Sistine Chapel ceiling frescoes

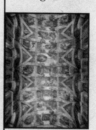

1524

Back in Florence, Michelangelo carves *Dawn and Dusk* for Lorenzo de Medici's tomb

1508

Pope Julius changes his mind and has Michelangelo start painting the ceiling of the Sistine Chapel

1510

1509

Henry, Prince of Wales, is crowned King Henry VIII of England at age 18

1517

Martin Luther posts his 95 theses on the door of the Palast Church in Wittenberg, beginning the Protestant Reformation in Germany

MICHELANGELO'S LIFE

1536

Michelangelo begins to paint *The Last Judgment* fresco in the Sistine Chapel

1545

Michelangelo paints another fresco, *The Conversion of Saint Paul,* for the Pauline Chapel in the Vatican

1526

Michelangelo completes *Day and Night* for Guiliano de Medici's tomb

1525

1540

1531

The "great comet," later called Halley's Comet, causes a wave of superstition

WORLD EVENTS

1546

Pope Paul III asks
Michelangelo to
complete St. Peter's
Basilica

1555

Michelangelo
destroys the
Florentine *Pietà*

1564

Michelangelo dies
on February 18,
1564, in Rome

1555

1558

Elizabeth I is
crowned in England,
beginning a 45-year
reign as queen

1545

The Catholic
Counter-Reformation
begins in Europe

FULL NAME: Michelangelo di Lodovico di Lionardo Buonarroti Simoni

DATE OF BIRTH: March 6, 1475

BIRTHPLACE: Caprese, Italy

FATHER: Lodovico Buonarroti

MOTHER: Francesca di Neri di Miniato del Sera Buonarroti

EDUCATION: Apprenticed with the painter Ghirlandaio

SPOUSE: none

DATE OF MARRIAGE: none

CHILDREN: none

DATE OF DEATH: February 18, 1564

PLACE OF BURIAL: Florence, Italy

In the Library

Connolly, Sean. *Michelangelo*. New York: World Almanac, 2004.

Corrain, Lucia. *The Art of the Renaissance*. New York: Peter Bedrick Books, 2001.

Milande, Veronique. *Michelangelo and His Times*. New York: Henry Holt & Company, Inc., 1996.

Pettit, Jayne. *Michelangelo: Genius of the Renaissance*. Danbury, Conn.: Franklin Watts, 1998.

Stanley, Diane. *Michelangelo*. New York: HarperCollins, 2000.

Additional Resources

On the Web

For more information on *Michelangelo*, use FactHound to track down Web sites related to this book.

1. Go to *www.facthound.com*
2. Type in a search word related to this book or this book ID: 0756508142
3. Click on the *Fetch It* button.

FactHound will find the best Web sites for you.

Historic Sites

Metropolitan Museum of Art
1000 Fifth Ave. at 82nd St.
New York, NY 10028
212/535-7710
To see a drawing by Michelangelo, as well as a portrait of him and a 1553 biography

National Gallery of Art
Constitution Avenue Northwest between Third and Seventh Streets
Washington, D.C. 20001
202/737-4215
To see three drawings by Michelangelo, as well as works by many of his peers

apprentice
a person who works for a skilled master to learn a trade or craft

cardinal
a high position in the Roman Catholic Church

commissions
projects, such as paintings, sculptures, or building designs, that are awarded to artists or craftsmen

conversion
a person's acceptance of a new religion

crucifixion
an execution carried out by nailing a person to a cross

ducats
the gold coins of Rome in Michelangelo's time

facade
a false front built onto an existing building

florins
the gold coins of Florence in Michelangelo's time

garlands
wreaths worn on the head for decoration

papal
under the control of or referring to the pope

patrons
people who sponsor artists, architects, writers, or other gifted people

restoration
to bring a work of art or other item back to its original condition

wet nurse
a woman hired to breast-feed another woman's child

Chapter 2

Page 15, line 12: Giorgio Vasari. *Lives of the Artists*. Translation by E. L. Seeley. NY: Farrar, Straus, and Giroux, 1957, p. 279.

Page 16, line 17: Ibid., p. 160.

Chapter 3

Page 25, sidebar: William E. Wallace. *Michelangelo: The Complete Sculpture, Painting, Architecture*. Hong Kong: Hugh Lauter Levin Associates, 1998, p. 13.

Chapter 4

Lives of the Artists, p. 289.

Page 31, line 6: Michelangelo Buonarroti. *Complete Poems and Selected Letters*. New York: Random House, 1963, p. 187.

Lives of the Artists, p. 292.

Chapter 5

Complete Poems and Selected Letters, pp. 191–192.

Chapter 6

Page 45, line 9: Gilles Néret. *Michelangelo*. New York: Barnes & Noble, 2001, p. 23.

Complete Poems and Selected Letters, p. 207.

Lives of the Artists, p. 301.

Page 51, line 15: Ibid.

Page 51, line 22: Michelangelo Buonarroti. *The Complete Poems of Michelangelo*. Translated by John Frederick Nims. Chicago: University of Chicago Press, 1998, #5.

Complete Poems and Selected Letters, p. 208.

Page 55, line 2: Ibid.

Lives of the Artists, p. 301.

Michelangelo, p. 46.

Chapter 7

Complete Poems and Selected Letters, pp. 223–224.

Michelangelo: The Complete Sculpture, Painting, Architecture, pp. 22, 24.

Michelangelo, p. 61.

Chapter 8

Michelangelo: The Compete Sculpture, Painting, Architecture, p. 27.

Page 75, line 4: "Final Days." *Michelangelo's Biography.* http://www.michelange-lo.com/buon/bio-final.html.

Michelangelo, p. 23.

Page 81, line 7: "Final Days." *Michelangelo's Biography.* http://www.michelange-lo.com/buon/bio-final.html.

Page 82, line 8: Michelangelo Buonarroti. "To Vittoria Colonna." Translated by Henry Wadsworth Longfellow. http://www.poetry-archive.com/b/to_vittoria_colonna.html.

Michelangelo: The Complete Sculpture, p. 28.

Page 87, line 21: Michelangelo Buonarroti. "On the Brink of Death." Translated by John Addington Symonds. http://www.poetry-archive.com/b/on_the_brink_of_death.html.

Page 89, line 6: "Final Days." *Michelangelo's Biography.* http://www.michelange-lo.com/buon/bio-final.html.

Chapter 9

Page 92, line 24: David Willey. "Sistine Chapel Restored." *BBC News.* December 11, 1999.

Page 95, line 5: Ibid.

Acidini, Cristina. *The Medici, Michelangelo, and the Art of Late Renaissance Florence*. New Haven, Conn.: Yale U. Press, 2002.

Beck, James H. *Three Worlds of Michelangelo*. New York: W. W. Norton & Co., 1999.

Bull, George Anthony. *Michelangelo: A Biography*. New York: St. Martin's Press, 1995.

Buonarroti, Michelangelo. *Complete Poems and Selected Letters*. New York: Random House, 1963.

Buonarroti, Michelangelo. *The Complete Poems of Michelangelo*. Translated by John Frederick Nims. Chicago: University of Chicago Press, 1998.

Hughes, Anthony. *Michelangelo*. London: Phaidon Press, 1997.

King, Ross. *Michelangelo and the Pope's Ceiling*. New York: Walker Publishing Company, 2003.

Néret, Gilles. *Michelangelo*. New York: Barnes & Noble, 2001.

Symonds, John Addington. *The Life of Michelangelo Buonarroti: Based on Studies in the Archives of the Buonarroti Family in Florence*. Philadelphia: University of Pennsylvania Press, 2002.

Vasari, Giorgio. *Lives of the Artists*. Translation by E. L. Seeley. New York: Farrar, Straus, and Giroux, 1957.

Wallace, William E. *Michelangelo: The Complete Sculpture, Painting, Architecture*. Hong Kong: Hugh Lauter Levin Associates, 1998.

Barbara A. Somervill has been writing for more than 30 years. She has written newspaper and magazine articles, video scripts, and books for children. She enjoys writing about science and investigating people's lives for biographies. She is an avid reader and traveler. Ms. Somervill lives with her husband in South Carolina.

Image Credits